A PHOTOGRAPHIC STUDY

Victoria

Steve Parish ™

Contents

▶▶

page 1: In autumn, carpets of multi-coloured leaves decorate Victorian streets and gardens as deciduous oaks, ashes, elms, poplars and planes prepare for winter. *pages 2 and 3:* The sand itself applauds the angler's success at Squeaky Beach, Wilsons Promontory. *pages 4 and 5:* Appropriately named "The Sentinels", potter Simon Rigg's bright ceramic statues "guard" the entrance to Crown Casino and the many shops and cinemas in the complex.

Introduction

▶ ▶

When the British Government decided to establish a penal colony at Botany Bay, the jewel of mainland Australia, the south-east, was unknown to them. Abel Tasman in 1644 had reached the west coast of Tasmania, and sailed south. James Cook in 1770 had reached the Australian coast at the point where the present border between New South Wales and Victoria reaches the sea, and sailed north.

The Henty family at Portland and Batman and Fawkner at Melbourne founded the colony of Victoria without government sanction from the parent colony in Sydney, and it was not until 1851 that London formalised the arrangement by appointing a Lieutenant-Governor and endorsing the colonists' choice of Victoria as a name.

But what a treasure they had gained! With reliable rainfall over most of its area, fertile soils, an equable climate and vast gold resources, Victoria was and is a very prosperous region. Smallest of the mainland states, it is second only to New South Wales in population and wealth. It is rich in visual delights, with towering forests and neat vineyards, snow-covered mountains and a rugged coastline.

Human activity has brought forth some wonders too. The capital, Melbourne, is a beautiful city where startling new structures blend with stately reminders of its history in a mixture which has always had an emphasis on people's needs. Ballarat and Bendigo, two of Australia's larger inland cities, have rich architectural heritages and vibrant futures. Both reflect the affluence brought by gold.

Victorians love sport, the arts and food. The Melbourne Cup and Australian Rules Football Grand Final, festivals of live performance and film, stylish restaurants – all are well attended in this very civilised state.

Over the years, it has been a pleasure to record on film the beauty of Victoria and the achievements of its people.

opposite: Green banks, shady trees, blue skies and reflected towers enhance rowing on the Yarra in summer.

Melbourne

▶▶

With more than three million residents, Melbourne is an important city by world standards – one with great wealth of natural and created beauty. The city's architecture is a stimulating mixture of old and new: on the one hand beautifully aged stone buildings in Parliament House, the General Post Office, the Town Hall and the imposing cathedrals, St Patricks and St Pauls, on the other startlingly modern Southgate, Federation Square and Crown Casino complex. A keen desire to preserve links with the past has resulted in the loving maintenance of significant buildings such as Old Melbourne Gaol, the elegant Princess Theatre and the Exhibition Building. That past was underwritten by the great riches wrested from the 19th Century goldfields.

The Zoological Gardens, Botanic Gardens, Fitzroy Gardens and Carlton Gardens are the most prominent of countless open areas which give the city such a sense of space. Much of the banks of the Yarra River, skirting and reflecting the city, has been beautifully landscaped. The river is important for recreation on its city reaches, and for trade nearer its mouth.

Melbourne is one of Australia's most pedestrian-friendly cities. All of the central retail area is easily explored on foot, and arts and entertainment facilities and restaurants lining the Yarra are within comfortable walking distance. Public transport, too, is excellent, with trams, buses and an electric train service, with an underground city loop.

Birthplace of Australian Rules football, Melbourne is a strong sporting centre. The mammoth Melbourne Cricket Ground (MCG), the Tennis Centre and Flemington Racecourse are but three of the hundreds of sporting venues. The annual AFL Grand Final in September, the Australian Open tennis in January, and the distance gallopers' pinnacle, the Melbourne Cup, on the first Tuesday of November, see the MCG, Melbourne Park and Flemington packed with enthusiastic crowds.

opposite: Flinders Street Station is a superb example of Edwardian baroque architecture. It is also an integral part of Melbourne's excellent public transport system. The comfortable modern tram gliding past is another.

pages 10 and 11: Federation Square is Melbourne's celebration of a century of national government. Beside startling art, it offers galleries, cinemas and restaurants. *page 11:* So typical of Melbourne's blend of old and new, an old clock on a cinema can be glimpsed from ultra-modern Federation Square.

above: The Cenotaph and the Eternal Flame (left) are expressions of respect for the past: the Crown Casino (right) an indication of hope for the future. *opposite:* This futuristic spire on the Victorian Arts Centre emphasises the ongoing importance of the arts to Victorians.

pages 14 and 15: The heart of Melbourne's central business district as viewed from the lofty heights of the Rialto Tower. page 16: Like London's traditional guardians, Melbourne's Gog and Magog watch over shoppers in the elegant Royal Arcade. page 17: An intricately ornate ceiling vaults over a former banking chamber in the Collins Street precinct.

WALK-THRU ~ SELF SERVE.

Queen Victoria
· M A R K E T ·

Available ON SUNDAYS

● MEAT - Full Range ● DELI
● FRUIT & VEGETABLES ● FISH

VALUE
#1.00

$2.50 KG

VALUE
#1.00

opposite: Lygon Street in Carlton is a mecca for diners, especially those with a taste for Italian food.
Melbourne's warm spring and summer make it ideal for the al fresco experience.
above: Melbourne boasts many markets where fresh produce is sold, of which the Queen Victoria Market, the
Prahran Market and the South Melbourne Market are perhaps the best known.

above, left: The cottage that belonged to Captain James Cook's parents has been faithfully rebuilt in the Fitzroy Gardens after transport from Yorkshire.

above, right: In the Old Melbourne Gaol, now a penal museum, Ned Kelly's famous armour is a prize exhibit.

above: The Princess Theatre has had more facelifts than an ageing star, but the last was wonderfully successful. Few would guess that this beauty is well over a hundred years old.

opposite: In Carlton Gardens stands the magnificent Royal Exhibition Building, completed in time for the 1880 Exhibition, and painstakingly maintained in all its glory. *above:* Complementing the Royal Exhibition Building in style is the Hochgurtel Fountain, named after its designer, Joseph Hochgurtel. *pages 24 and 25:* Fitzroy Gardens are mostly open space, but its renowned conservatory houses more formal elements.

pages 26 and 27: As night falls over the glass-like stillness of the Yarra waters, the last glow of the clouds is reflected along with the lights of the city. *page 28:* Pleasure and fishing craft shelter in calm waters at St Kilda. *page 29:* Old but very much alive is Luna Park, St Kilda's historic amusement ground.

above, left: Tennis is served up at the Australian Open at Melbourne Park. *above, right:* An aerial battle is an appropriate Australian Rules contest between Bombers and Crows. *opposite:* With a huge playing surface and Colosseum-like grandstands almost encircling the arena, the Melbourne Cricket Ground (MCG) is home to the Australian Football League Grand Final, cricket Test Matches and other international sporting events.

above: Part of the field, usually of 24 horses, as the Flemington barrier stalls fly open at the start of the 3200-metre Melbourne Cup, Australia's richest and best known horse race.
opposite: At the spring race meetings, especially the day of the Oaks Stakes for 3-year-old fillies, women's fashions draw almost as much attention as the horses.

Melbourne's Shorelines

▶ ▶

Vast and shallow, Port Phillip Bay is divided into smaller bays by a series of peninsulas and headlands, of which the Mornington and Bellarine Peninsulas are the most prominent.

Mornington Peninsula reaches south and west between Port Phillip Bay and Western Port. From the Yarra mouth east down the coast, Hobsons Bay, St Kilda (slightly raffish and very cosmopolitan) and Brighton lead to the fashionable peninsular beaches, notably Dromana, Sorrento and Portsea. From the historic bathing boxes at Brighton to the grand houses and boathouses nearer the southern tip the emphasis is on pleasure. Restaurants often serve local food and wine. Beyond the beaches strong seas pound the coast from Point Nepean and Cape Schanck to West Head.

On the western shore of Port Phillip Bay, Williamstown is a revitalised port area very close to Melbourne. Steeped in history, it is also a modish residential area for modern living. Early railway construction gave this shore of Port Phillip Bay easy access to Melbourne's growing market for meat, dairy and poultry products and fruit and vegetables.

On Corio Bay stands the major port of Geelong, an important exporter of wheat, wool and meat, and Victoria's second largest city. Nearby are manufacturing and refining facilities. Geelong is home to an old National Trust-classified bluestone wool store brilliantly recycled as the National Wool Museum. Other splendid buildings in the area include Werribee Park Mansion, with its sixty handsome rooms, and ornate hotels at Queenscliff, near the tip of Bellarine Peninsula.

From Queenscliff a ferry runs to Sorrento on the Mornington Peninsula. The 35-minute trip inside the bay brings passengers safely close to the notorious Rip, where the waters of broad sea and sheltered bay surge and boil with the changing tides.

opposite: The shores of Port Phillip Bay are dotted with jetties, and strolling on them or the sandy shores is one of Melburnians' great pleasures.

above: Along with many other bayside beaches, Brighton is enlivened by brightly
coloured historic bathing boxes, eagerly sought and carefully preserved.

above: A Williamstown jetty is crowded with moored and landed boats and a restaurant.

page 40: Yachts and other pleasure craft ride at anchor with the city's skyscrapers in the background. page 41: Bathed in sunlight, refurbished old buildings find a new lease of life in the age of kerbside dining.

opposite: At the western end of Mornington Peninsula, Point Nepean stretches a sandy finger toward Point Lonsdale and Geelong. *above:* Boardwalk and railings guide sightseers to the stark beauty of Cape Schanck at the extreme southern tip of Mornington Peninsula. *pages 44 and 45:* The grand notions of 19th Century British settlers find expression in Werribee Mansion.

pages 46 and 47: In downtown Geelong, the old Sailor's Rest building now houses a restaurant. In the foreground is part of the growing outdoor art collection that is bringing grace and beauty to the busy city. *pages 48 and 49:* In a public park in Geelong, 2-metre-high, brightly painted bollards, created by Jan Mitchell, recall brass bands of the past.

above, far left: The Point Lonsdale Lighthouse on Bellarine Peninsula helps to guide shipping through the dangerous waters of The Rip at Port Phillip Heads.
above: Many bayside beaches sport a jetty, often originally an aid to local water traffic, now a place for promenade or fishing.

opposite: The approaches to Queenscliff's waterfront are
enhanced by this lovely old building, the Hotel Royal.
above: Typical 19th Century iron lace adds beauty to these solid
old houses at Queenscliff.

The Yarra Valley and the Dandenongs

The Yarra River is Melbourne's artery, and the Dandenongs are its lungs. The Yarra flows from the southern slopes of the Great Dividing Range through Melbourne to Port Phillip Bay. The Yarra Valley proper stretches from Yarra Junction to Lower Plenty, but the name is more widely used. Once, Healesville Sanctuary and its wildlife was the valley's chief claim to fame, together with its being the birthplace of Nellie Mitchell, better known as the great Australian soprano, Dame Nellie Melba.

The Yarra Valley first produced fine wines in the 19th Century, with those of the Swiss winemakers, the de Castella brothers at St Hubert's and Baron de Pury at Yerinberg particularly prized. Fashions change, and by the early 20th Century, the industry had all but died. In recent years, improved techniques have re-established its reputation as an important cool climate producer of excellent table wines.

In the Dandenong Ranges, lyrebirds, parrots, bellbirds, koalas, kangaroos and bandicoots move among giant eucalypts and feathery tree ferns. Moisture and warmth encourage plant growth, and nurseries abound in the Dandenongs. Private gardens are tended with care, but none can surpass the National Rhododendron Gardens at Olinda. Fruit growing, too, is a major industry in the Dandenongs, especially of berry fruits.

The moderate climate and relative proximity to Melbourne have attracted many commuters who enjoy both worlds, the advantages of the city and the beauty of the mountains.

No description of the area would be complete without reference to Puffing Billy, the tiny old steam locomotive that pulls slowly through the bush old-style carriages packed with tourists. It travels over timber trestle bridges more than 100 years old as it makes its way from Belgrave to the delightfully named Gembrook.

opposite: The hot air balloon is advertising an interstate product, but the Yarra Valley itself is one of Australia's most highly regarded producers of fine table wines. *page 56:* Exotic and native plants create a harmonious scene in the Dandenong Ranges. *page 57:* Olinda is the home of the National Rhododendron Gardens, where many associated genera also flourish.

above: Two sculptures by William Ricketts, the remarkable 20th Century untrained artist, flank a typical Sherbrooke Forest scene.

above: Delight of visitors, the old steam excursion train hauled by tiny
Puffing Billy bustles its way through the Dandenongs.

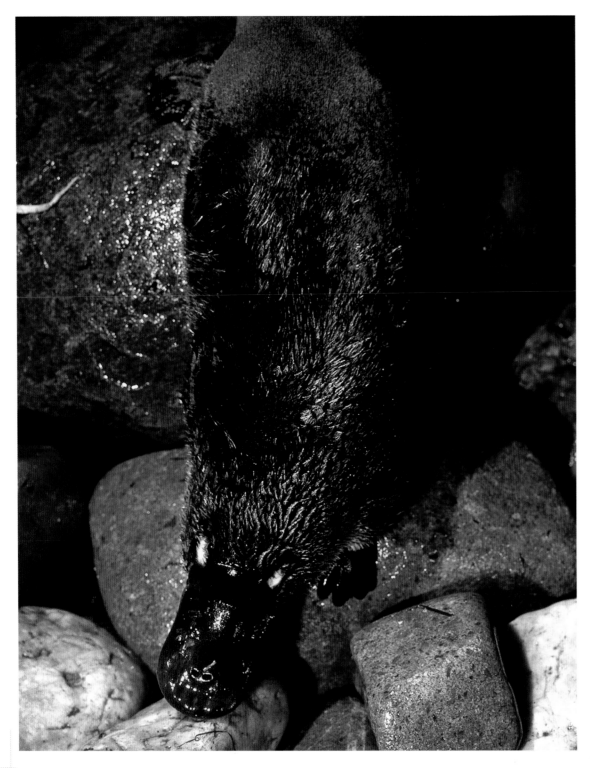

above: Two of the special locals in the hills outside Melbourne, the bizarre Platypus and Nature's mimic, the Superb Lyrebird.
opposite: With huge eucalypts behind them shedding bark in long strips, the tree ferns give a sense of moister ages.

above, left: The pretty creeper *Hardenbergia violacea* has acquired a number of common names, of which False Sarsaparilla is perhaps the most popular.

above, centre: Mist shrouds the forest in the Yarra Ranges.
above, right: The Rush-leaf wattle.

East of Melbourne

The eastern region of Victoria is cool, wet and highly productive. It is also a wonderful vacation and touring area.

On Phillip Island, lying across the entrance to Western Port, swimming, surfing, sailing and fishing are common pursuits, while for the more terrestrial, watching the annual Australian 500 cc Motor Cycle Grand Prix and bushwalking are options. The island also has colonies of Australian Fur-seals, Koalas and Little Penguins.

Much of Wilsons Promontory, Victoria's southernmost point, is national park. Near Yarram, a charming old town, the small Tarra–Bulga National Park displays cool temperate rainforest, notably enormous Mountain Ash trees, and Myrtle Beech and tree ferns.

In East Gippsland, dairy, meat and timber continue as major industries, but the wonderful coastline and waterways, the rugged high country, and extensive parks and reserves make the region an important tourist destination. Lakes Entrance, for example, which is also a commercial fishing port, is popular with holiday-makers.

The large coastal Croajingolong National Park provides access to Mallacoota for fishing, and to the Point Hicks lighthouse. This busy coast sees much of the mercantile shipping working through Victoria's major ports, and lighthouses are common along the sometimes treacherous coastline.

Further inland, trees, horses and cattle tend to dominate lives. In Snowy River country, working horses and thoroughbreds are highly prized. Eastern Victorian country centres host many race meetings.

The Latrobe Valley provides a contrast. Its rich brown coal deposits have led to the establishment of large centres in Moe, Morwell and Traralgon. It is home to Victoria's major power generation facilities.

Near the industrial area, intensive dairy farming takes advantage of the good rainfall. Gourmet cheeses are increasingly in evidence in this region. Vineyards, too, have spread in South Gippsland and high quality wines are important in the regional economy.

opposite: Perched high on Mount Oberon on Wilsons Promontory, visitors have an extended view of Bass Strait.

opposite: Cape Woolamai, the southernmost tip of Phillip Island, is forbidding from the sea and awe-inspiring from the land. *above, left:* Even under threatening skies and with a strong surf pounding, this beach on Phillip Island has a welcoming charm. *above, right:* Little Penguins burrow and breed on the sand dunes of the island, much to the delight of visitors.

opposite: This dramatic aerial photograph of rugged and pounding seas underlines the need for caution off the south coast of Phillip Island.
above: The Nobbies, Phillip Island's quaintly named and strangely shaped formation, stand out against the gold of the setting sun.

above, left: In Gippsland, the line of smoke stacks in the
background contrasts with fertile farmland.
above, right: Gently undulating paddocks provide rich pastures
for Gippsland's many dairy herds.

above: Giant eucalypts are a feature of the Tarra–Bulga
National Park, north of the town of Yarram.

opposite: The Star Hotel in the Gippsland town of Sale is a splendid reminder of the colonial period, very much fully operational as a 21st Century establishment.
above: The old Yarram Courthouse has been refurbished and now serves as a tourist centre.

above: Part of the commercial fishing fleet moored at Lakes Entrance.

above: Australian Pelicans have learned that waiting for the fishing boats' return is easier than fishing.

opposite: The town of Lakes Entrance and the system of Gippsland lakes and rivers from the air.
above: To the left of the channel at Lakes Entrance stretch the dunes of Gippsland Lakes Coastal Park.
pages 78 and 79: Seabirds gather in the shallows of the Tidal River on Wilsons Promontory.
pages 80 and 81: Wilsons Promontory Lighthouse warns ships in Bass Strait of ever-present danger.

opposite: A kangaroo takes time off from feeding among the wind-twisted tree trunks.
above, left: The beautiful *Banksia ericifolia* inflorescence brightens the bushland.
above, centre: An Eastern Grey kangaroo belies the name, glowing gold at change of light.
above, right: Pink Heath, the floral symbol of Victoria.

above: Victoria's wild east coast has sandy and rocky beaches to delight the eye.
opposite: Lieutenant Zachary Hicks on Cook's *Endeavour* was honoured in the naming of Point Hicks, where this lighthouse and lighthouse keepers' cottages now stand in Croajingolong National Park.

The High Country

▶ ▶

Most of Victoria's snowfields are in the Alpine National Park, which at 6460 square kilometres is the state's largest. The snow-capped mountains and ski resorts of this region are among the most popular in the nation. Easily reached and seasonally reliable, they form Victoria's winter playground. Especially at Mt Buffalo, Mt Hotham and Falls Creek, skiers from all over the country gather for their sport from June to October.

In summer other interests prevail, with bushwalking, birdwatching, nature photography and fishing in the pure water of the upland streams high on the list of favourites. Both flora and fauna include numbers of species rare or absent elsewhere, including the Mountain Pygmy-possum. Above the treeline, alpine meadows come alive with colour as spring advances, and sparkling streamlets of melting snow moisten the beds of sphagnum moss and peat.

Scenery is on the grand scale, with deep valleys and grassy meadowland. The main population centres are mostly on significant streams: Wangaratta sits beside the River Ovens and Wodonga beside the River Murray. The Great Alpine Road winds though Myrtleford and Bright to Mt Beauty. To the east Omeo gives access to the Bogong Plateau.

Although well east of the major goldfields, Beechworth was a centre for alluvial gold panning. Its 19th Century buildings have been carefully preserved, including the courthouse in which the outlaw Ned Kelly twice faced trial.

The region is an important food supplier. Cattle and sheep graze through the lower areas. Several wineries, including a large one at Milawa, flourish here, and gourmet suppliers are increasingly important. Culinary tourism is a growing industry in the region.

opposite: Recalling Banjo Paterson's much loved poem "The Man from Snowy River", these horses and riders of the high country are on the upper reaches of the River Murray at Tom Groggin.
pages 88 and 89: Old buildings and streetscapes such as this in the former gold seeking centre of Beechworth justify the National Trust's decision to classify the whole town.

pages 90 and 91: On the upper reaches of the River Murray near Biggara.
above: At its eastern end, poplars are often found lining the Murray Valley Highway.

above: The old Omeo Post Office was obviously built to withstand the winter chills.
pages 94 and 95: Snow-clad slopes near Mt Hotham in the Great Dividing Range.

opposite: At high altitudes, alpine eucalypts produce natural sculptures as they struggle against the elements. *above, left:* A wombat sniffs cautiously. *above, centre:* The brilliant balls of wattle blossom brighten the alpine scene. *above, right:* A Gang-gang Cockatoo huddles against the cold.

pages 98 and 99: **In the fresh alpine air over Mt Hotham the setting sun brings brilliant colour.**

above: Nestling in a broad valley, Bright displays autumn foliage in contrast to the deep green of native trees.

opposite: In the High Country the autumn foliage of deciduous exotic trees is particularly vivid. *above:* This street scene reflects Bright's civic pride. *page 104:* Trees in the mist on Mt Buffalo. *pages 104 and 105:* Fascinating cloud formations over Mt Buffalo.

North of Melbourne

▶ ▶

Wheat, wool, dairy produce, fruit and wine are in abundance in this fertile area of Victoria's Spa Country, Goldfields and Goulburn-Murray Waters. Natural, mineral-rich springs in the area led early British settlers to liken it to some of the famous spas in their former homeland, such as Bath. Among others, Hepburn Springs has retained this reputation.

The springs and some curious land formations, such as the vertical basalt pillars in Organ Pipes National Park, are legacies of prehistoric volcanic activity. Mt Macedon (1013 metres) and Hanging Rock are other notable formations in the region. Nowadays, horse, sheep and cattle studs, vineyards and orchards prosper.

The Goulburn River rises in the Great Dividing Range and feeds the Eildon storage before meandering through the towns of Nagambie, Seymour and Shepparton, finally joining the Murray at a point a little to the east of the old river port of Echuca. It has great economic importance. Shepparton is the centre of a major fruit canning industry.

The great gold centres of Ballarat and Bendigo continue to prosper, but without the riotous behaviour of the gold rush days. The Eureka Stockade at Ballarat saw miners and police troopers in battle against each other on the 3rd of December, 1854, because of alleged harassment and excessive taxation of miners. Sovereign Hill, a faithful re-creation of gold rush days in Ballarat, gives a convincing insight into that life.

Both Bendigo and Ballarat had electric tram services. Bendigo maintains some tracks along which tourist trams run.

Picturesque Daylesford, a preferred "smallish town" background for television producers, has links with both Goldfields and the Spa Country.

Throughout the large region, wine has become an important industry, and styles range from rich fortified wines in the north to elegant table wines in the Pyrenees.

opposite: Cattle graze contentedly in lush pastures near Seymour in Central Victoria.

above: Oil seed and fodder crops thrive in the flat paddocks near Shepparton in the north of the Goulburn Valley.

opposite: Smaller than its goldfields neighbours, Ararat nonetheless has a rich heritage of buildings from the Victorian era.
above: Many Victorian towns have large, beautiful railway stations. This one is in Maryborough.

above: Verandahs provide shelter from winter rains and
summer heat in mid-town Ballarat.

above: Inside the Robert Clark Conservatory in the Ballarat Botanic Gardens, elegant statuary stands amid delicate blooms.

above and opposite: Sovereign Hill in Ballarat provides living reminders of life in a gold town more than 150 years ago.

above: The little town of Rutherglen in the north-east is the centre for one of Australia's oldest and most respected wine areas.

above: Wangaratta is a bustling rural and manufacturing centre
on the banks of the Ovens River.

pages 118 and 119: Trentham Falls in Wombat State Forest
have the state's highest clear drop.

above: A bridge over placid waters in Daylesford. The area is famed for the
rejuvenating effects of its springs and spas.

pages 122 and 123: Emphasising the region's renowned mineral waters,
an ornate fountain stands near the centre of Daylesford.
opposite: PS (paddlesteamer) *Emmylou* cruises out of Echuca, powered by wood-fired boilers.
above: A houseboat at Echuca.

pages 126 and 127: Lake Mulwala, a body of River Murray water between Yarrawonga (Victoria) and Mulwala (NSW) held back by the Yarrawonga Weir, reflects the fiery sun.

above: Near Wodonga the River Murray, until the late 19th Century a major transport artery for traders, shows life and freshness.

The Great Ocean Road

Some rugged and spectacular coastline lies along this highway, but there are many favourite resort towns and trade and manufacturing centres too. Officially running from Torquay in the east to Warrnambool in the west, it is extended in popular usage to the border with South Australia.

From Aireys Inlet to Kennett River the road is very winding and although passengers in vehicles may enjoy the blue of the sea and the many cliffs and limestone stacks, such as the celebrated Twelve Apostles, drivers are advised to concentrate on the road.

Lighthouses have been essential on this rocky coast, especially before radio and radar aids to mariners, and the section traversed by the Great Ocean Road retains many splendid examples.

Popular coastal resort towns, Lorne, Apollo Bay and Port Campbell, are backed by the Otway Ranges, where huge Tasmanian Blue Gums and Australian Beech (*Nothofagus*) tower.

Port Fairy with its 19th Century buildings and brightly painted commercial fishing fleet serves its hinterland primary producers and others as a captivating holiday spot.

Warrnambool and Portland are industrial centres, and appropriately between them stands Victoria's first wind farm for generating electricity. Both, especially Portland, are also important shipping centres serving their own considerable populations and the highly productive pastoral and agricultural regions behind them.

Another interesting aspect of the area is that recent archaeological research has found apparent stone hut walls and stone eel traps carbon-dated to about 8000 years old at Lake Condah near Heywood. It is highly likely that the Aboriginal people of this area, unlike those of less benevolent parts of Australia, lived in permanent dwellings and subsisted on the local food. It is thought likely that they traded produce from their labours prior to European settlement.

opposite: Near the delightful old hamlet of Aireys Inlet, the Split Point Lighthouse reassures mariners that they have successfully rounded Cape Otway.

pages 132 and 133: Warm sand and a gentle ocean swell – what
more could a pair of children want?

above: Rocks torn from the cliffs by the sea are scattered along the beach near Anglesea.
pages 136 and 137: A comfortable dog on the beach epitomises Lorne's great appeal
– lazy days in a very beautiful and hospitable spot.

above, top: Apollo Bay township curling idly around its crescent beach
is in reality a busy commercial fishing and dairying centre.
above, bottom: Fishing boats at anchor in Apollo Bay.

above: The narrow western entrance to Bass Strait known as the Eye of the Needle was for many years made safer by the Cape Otway Lighthouse, now decommissioned and replaced by a solar-powered light.

opposite, above and following: Travellers on the Great Ocean Road can gaze in wonder at the group of limestone stacks known, regardless of their number, as the Twelve Apostles.

above: A short journey east of the township of Beech Forest in the Otway Ranges, dense cool temperate rainforest frames Hopetoun Falls.

pages 146 and 147: Fishing boats lie at anchor in the River Moyne in the lovely old coastal town of Port Fairy, a favourite holiday spot.

above, left: Pleasure boats ready for service at Warrnambool.
above, right: Gazing down a major business street in Warrnambool.

above, left: Part of Warrnambool's waterfront, with Lady Bay Lower Lighthouse in the background.
above, right: The Lady Bay Upper Lighthouse on Flagstaff Hill can be lined up with the lower one to guide shipping into Lady Bay.

West of Melbourne

▶ ▶

The Grampians, or Gariwerd as they are known to local Aborigines, are a series of predominantly sandstone ranges rising abruptly from the surrounding flat farmlands. Some of the area, notably near Zumstein, is formed from granite, and has gentler topography than the deeply weathered sandstone.

Much favoured for bushwalking, rock-climbing and vacations, the mountains have a practical side too. Their streams have been dammed to provide water storage for this drier corner of Victoria, with more than fifty cities and towns relying on these storages for water.

Gariwerd is rich in native fauna and flora, some species being restricted to this area. Carpets of colourful wildflowers are at their best in spring. With many of the mammals and reptiles shy, nocturnal or both, birdlife is more frequently seen. Waterbirds, raptors, parrots and songbirds are much in evidence, and with such a rich flora, honeyeaters are everywhere. Forest eucalypts and wattles, heathland peas, grevilleas and banksias all attract birds.

Aborigines have lived in the region for more than five thousand years, and there are more Aboriginal rock art sites here than anywhere else in south-east Australia.

Beyond the Grampians the rich Wimmera grain belt stretches into the remoter country. Victoria is too compact and favoured to have much outback, but there are some lonely stretches between Hopetoun and the Sturt Highway. In the middle of this area there is a string of small towns along the Mallee Highway linking Ouyen with the South Australian mallee country.

In the north, flat dry land is still useful in most parts for grain or livestock. River Murray water allows irrigation for vineyards and orchards. Down from the mountains, the river presents a different character, with broad, sweeping bends and small islands. The beautiful city of Mildura is the "capital" of the north-west. In the west, too, are the nearest thing that Victoria has to a desert in the Little Desert. In the semi-arid country of the Big Desert and the Sunset Country, reptiles rule the sand dunes, birds the skies, and vegetation is hardy to survive baking summer heat and freezing winter nights.

opposite: This view from Mount William in the Grampians shows characteristic weathering.

opposite: Beneath the ridges in the Grampians large grassy flats are dotted with spreading gums.
These are natural feeding areas for kangaroos and wallabies.
above, left: In winter, myriad waterfalls trill or thunder from the sandstone and granite ridges.
above, right: The track through the gorge known as the Grand Canyon is very popular with bushwalkers.

above: Spread about the meandering Murray in its mature stage, Mildura reflects
the prosperity the river has brought to the region.

above: Mildura's former library is now called the Carnegie Centre, and houses the Mildura Historical Society and the Genealogical Society. Its clocktower is a landmark in Deakin Avenue.

opposite: A typical Wimmera scene shows a grain planting stretching over huge flat paddocks, dotted with remnants of the original eucalypt forest. *above, left:* A River Red Gum spreads across soil and water. *above, centre:* In the mallee country, bright flowers of mallee species from many parts of Australia have been planted. *above, right:* Wind and water sculpt the dunes in the Sunset Country.

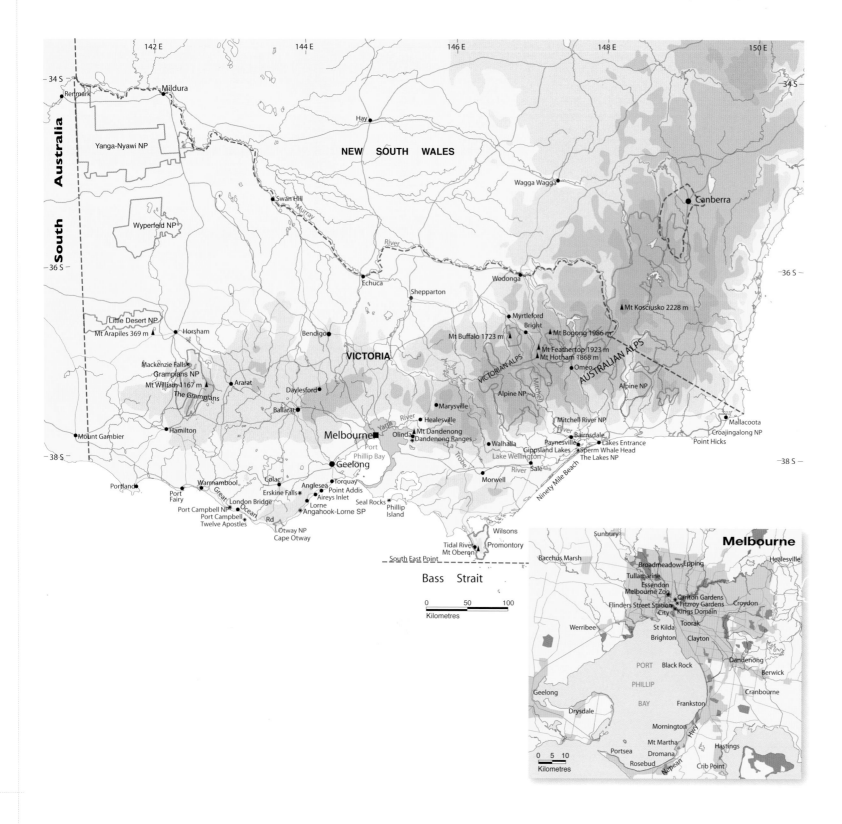

South Australia

142 E
144 E
146 E
148 E
150 E

34 S
34 S

Renmark
Mildura

Yanga-Nyawi NP

NEW SOUTH WALES

Hay

36 S

Swan Hill
Murray

Wyperfeld NP

River

Wagga Wagga
Canberra

Echuca
Shepparton
Wodonga
Mt Kosciusko 2228 m

Little Desert NP
Horsham
Bendigo
Myrtleford
Bright
Mt Buffalo 1723 m
Mt Bogong 1986 m

Mt Arapiles 369 m
VICTORIA
Mt Featherop 1923 m
Mt Hotham 1868 m

Mackenzie Falls
Grampians NP
Mt William 1167 m
Ararat
Daylesford
VICTORIAN ALPS
Omeo
AUSTRALIAN ALPS
Alpine NP

The Grampians
Ballarat
Alpine NP
Mitchell
Mallacoota

Hamilton
Marysville
Mitchell River NP
Croajingalong NP

Mount Gambier
Melbourne
Healesville
River
Bairnsdale
Point Hicks

36 S

38 S
Olinda
Mt Dandenong
Dandenong Ranges
Paynesville
Lakes Entrance
Sperm Whale Head
The Lakes NP
38 S

Port Phillip Bay
Walhalla
Gippsland Lakes
Lake Wellington

Geelong
La Trobe
Sale

Portland
Warrnambool
Colac
Torquay
Morwell
River
Ninety Mile Beach

Port Fairy
Erskine Falls
Anglesea
Point Addis
Aireys Inlet

London Bridge
Great
Lorne
Seal Rocks

Port Campbell NP
Ocean
Angahook-Lorne SP
Phillip Island

Port Campbell
Twelve Apostles
Rd
Otway NP
Cape Otway
Wilsons Promontory

Tidal River
Mt Oberon
South East Point

Bass Strait

0   50   100
Kilometres

Melbourne

Sunbury
Healesville

Bacchus Marsh
Broadmeadows
Epping

Tullamarine
Essendon
Melbourne Zoo
Carlton Gardens
Fitzroy Gardens
Croydon
Flinders Street Station
City
Kings Domain

Werribee
St Kilda
Toorak

Brighton
Clayton

PORT
PHILLIP
Black Rock
Dandenong
Berwick

BAY
Frankston
Cranbourne

Geelong

Drysdale
Mornington

Mt Martha
Hastings

Portsea
Dromana
HWY

Rosebud
Crib Point

N-pean

0 5 10
Kilometres

1	Melbourne's Shorelines
2	Yarra Valley & Dandenongs
3	East of Melbourne
4	The High Country
5	North of Melbourne
6	Great Ocean Road
7	West of Melbourne

Mildura

7

Echuca
5

VICTORIA
4

Ballarat
2

6
MELBOURNE
3

Warrnambool
1
Wilsons Promontory

BASS STRAIT

Index

above: Looking from bottom left, over the suburbs of Middle Park and Albert Park and Albert Park Lake, with the Albert Park Public Golf Course at top right, and the South Melbourne skyline in the distance.

Published by Steve Parish Publishing Pty Ltd
PO Box 1058, Archerfield, Queensland 4108 Australia

www.steveparish.com.au

© copyright Steve Parish Publishing Pty Ltd
ISBN 174021569 9

Photography: Steve Parish

p.13: Ian Roberts

Additional photography:
pp.14–5: Ian Roberts; p.18, 19: David Simmonds; p.20, right: Pat Slater; p.30 left: Tom Putt, Sport the Library; p.30 right: Sport the Library; p.32: Jacki Ames, Sport the Library; p.33, Robin Smith, photolibrary.com; p.54–5: R. Ian Lloyd

Public art: Jan Mitchell, Baywalk Bollards: pp. 48–9

Text: Neil Lovett
Proofreading: Debra Hudson
Design: Leanne Staff

Maps supplied by MAPGraphics, Australia
Printed in China by Printplus Limited
Film by Colour Chiefs, Brisbane, Australia

Produced in Australia at the Steve Parish Publishing Studios